This Paper Boat follows the author as he traces his own history through the lives and written fragments of Iris Wilkinson (aka Robin Hyde), of his parents and their parents. He explores old territories of Robin Hyde's, still dripping with the past – the tide pool at Island Bay with its shrimp and driftwood, the garden at Laloma with its crushed lemon leaves. He listens to family stories, the eels and milk, frangipani trees, drains and barbed wire of his parents' childhoods. He remembers a jungle of his own; he searches for ghosts in the water. While stumbling across irreparable fractures between worlds, the author uncovers the permission to have beautiful and imperfect plans.

Gregory Kan is a writer based in Auckland. His work has been featured in literary journals such as *brief*, *Hue & Cry*, *Minarets*, *otoliths*, *Percutio*, *Sport* and *Turbine*, as well as contemporary art exhibitions, journals and catalogues. An earlier incarnation of *This Paper Boat* was shortlisted for the Kathleen Grattan Poetry Prize in 2013.

This Paper Boat

Gregory Kan

AUCKLAND
UNIVERSITY
PRESS

In this sequence, I have sampled from the writings of Iris Wilkinson, better known under her alias, Robin Hyde. A list of the works drawn from follows the sequence.

The apparition or figuration of Hyde is sometimes indicated in the short, as 'I.' But I also like to think that she, and the other ghosts, can be found in all the white spaces of these poems.

Outside the square of land you last appeared on
seventy-five years ago, I pretend to busy
my phone. I am

taking in the way Wellington had to force itself
upwards to meet you, who always seemed to be waiting
at the top of stairs. At the gate, I peer

into the front garden, my back to the bend of the road, a position
from which no passing car or pedestrian
can see me. You can be found.

I have to hear you to keep you
here, and I have to keep you
here to keep coming back.

It is sometimes the least
personal thing, to want to renew one's openness
to the outside.

The name of the house was a Samoan word, *Laloma*, meaning 'The Abode of Love'. Iris Wilkinson, the poet and scholar of the family, occupied the top room, which looked out on to hills kindled with gorse. I. remembered her mother below, at her old sewing machine, which broke the thread so often it taxed her patience. Her children's frocks were always the prettiest, though her sight had begun to blur behind her spectacles. Young seedlings grow up through the adult gorse, cutting out its light and eventually replacing it. Most methods of destroying adult gorse plants have been found to create the ideal conditions for gorse seeds to germinate.

At Island Bay, I look from tide pool to the moon and then back
to the tide pool. I realise
that you couldn't have been catching shrimp big enough

to eat
but small enough to contain, in large numbers, in old
marmalade jars. When prying driftwood from the sand, I smell

crushed lemon leaves. I don't know anything about
the past except
for what the past has left me.

The handle on the driver's door of my car is broken,
so I have to climb over
from the passenger seat.

Origin of *garden*: Middle English *gardin*, from Anglo-French *gardin*, *jardin*, of Germanic origin; akin to Old High German *gart* – an enclosure. The words *yard*, *court* and Latin *hortus* all refer to an enclosed space. Love has to be kept away from the world. After meeting him for the first time, I. watched Harry leave the garden through a hole in the back fence, under the ngaio tree. She stood crumpling the pale lemon leaves in her fingers, their scent creeping out into the skin of her palms. The stream came down in a waterfall, to a pool nearly six feet deep. There was a huge boulder in the middle of it, where she could sit.

Looking down at my boots I couldn't tell whether I was in Singapore, New Zealand, Thailand or Brunei. All dirt tracks look the same to me, at night. The gradual accumulation of sediment. Crouched beside the track, I ate biscuits to try to stay awake. When we began moving again I watched one of my platoon-mates stumble off the track, in sleep. The sediment is compacted as more and more material is deposited on top. Walking through Wilton's Bush a few days ago I was disoriented when I cut my hand on a thorny, overhanging branch. I realised I had no gloves. No camouflage paint on my face, no equipment vest, no rifle around my neck, no ammunition, no water, no signal set, no platoon, no rank. Eventually the underlying sediment becomes so dense it is essentially rock.

My parents always ask me when I'm coming back
with all that coming back
can presuppose.

On the plane to Auckland
I worry about what to ask them.
I ask these questions, not so that I can

write, but I write so that I can ask these questions. I worry that my parents' answers are just another thing that I will be taking from them.

The two men sitting next to me
discuss the construction and regulation
of fences.

At the dining table my mother speaks
readily but I wish she would trust
her recollections more.

As she talks, she looks off
to the right, where her Bible study notes have
amassed like leaves against the roots of a tree.

There are details I know she has hidden
from me. It is difficult to see my time
as removed or separate from that of my

parents'. I draw the boughs
downwards in the thickets
behind her eyes. A verbal tic, she cycles

through my siblings'
names – Joel, Sarah – before she gets to mine.

When my mother began attending school she didn't know her name. Her family used to call her *Ah Nia* or *Nia Kia*, which translate as 'small one' or 'small child'. Being small she was often seated at the front of the class. She tells me that she wasn't very clever, but that she was helpful and obedient and that teachers liked her.

Drainage is important in Singapore, and at the time no drains were covered. There was a drain that ran across her garden, emptying itself eventually into a large canal. She heard reports of children swept away in periods of heavy rainfall. She doesn't know where the canal led. Drifting trees and dead dogs when water levels were high. She remembers talking with her sisters for hours, with their feet pushed against one bank of the drain and their backs against the other. They sometimes crawled through drains to reach the other side of the road, below the increasingly heavy and unsteady traffic.

When my father was a child, he would fish in drains that cut across his village. Sometimes the rain fell heavily enough for eels to be found in the larger drains. Sitting where the drain disappeared into the ground, a hooked worm swinging from a strip of coconut leaf in his hands. The biggest eel he ever caught was one and a half feet long. He hunted eel and fish in drains until he was fourteen or fifteen years old.

Wherever he was with his friends, they would look out for tembusu trees, and they would look out for the perfectly symmetrical fork of a branch. The slingshot he gave me when I was seven was smooth and varnished. The trunk of a tembusu tree is dark brown, with deeply fissured bark. The best ammunition is a glass marble, he tells me, because it is perfectly round, and this perfect roundness ensures the consistency of its flight.

There was a book of animal stories on my bedside table. He said: You can hold in such a way that the air is trapped between your hand and the water. My father stepped into a clearing with me on his shoulders. We were in an upward tug of forest. He said: By relieving the pressure exerted by your hand you can release the air at whatever rate you desire. We were moving at a distance from the water. Where we were it was green and tufted.

I spoke but I was not sure if my room-mate was awake. I was barely eighteen when I got there and I would be twenty by the time I left. Our room was furthest from the toilet and I tried to stay asleep even as I parted the hallway lights. After a few months I became too tired to have a temper. I dipped the rag in black shoe polish, and then in water. I had developed a different accent and a hunger for chimes in the darkness that only I could hear. My mother used to make up stories in the darkness that no one knew the endings to. It was a kind of permission to have imperfect and beautiful plans.

I went a few times with my mother
to visit her at the rest home.
As a child I knew her as my great-aunt.

She had lost most of her memory. Every visit she asked
my mother what her 'position' was, and every visit
my mother told her that she, my mother, was the seventh

of nine children. This was how my great-aunt recognised
my mother or my mother's siblings, who
were my great-aunt's only visitors.

She would ask my mother to walk her around the garden.

She woke often
in the middle of the night, screaming
for the staff to wash her. Before being admitted

to the rest home, my great-aunt stayed with my aunt Vivian, who
was the sixth of nine. Vivian found her, one night, washing
dishes in the toilet.

She fell twice in one night. Not knowing what else
to do, my aunt and uncle considered
tying her to the bed. She sometimes

repulsed me. I remember that when hugging her I wondered
what made her skin so
detached from her flesh.

She had kind,
sad eyes. Her funeral was simple. The pastor spoke in Teochew.

My mother tells me that my great-aunt was actually
my grandfather's first wife. He had moved
to Singapore for work, leaving her

in Guangzhou. He did not think
he would ever see her again.

My mother does not know how
my great-aunt made her way to Singapore. She arrived
to find my grandfather,

his new wife, and children. My grandfather and grandmother did not stay
at the house, but at the Chinese medicine shop
they operated.

My great-aunt lived with and took care of
my mother and her siblings for the rest
of her life.

She had no other friends or family in Singapore. She used to bathe
the children in rainwater
collected in a giant urn outside the house. The water was

always cold. Intensity
plays a fundamental role in the formation
of memory. Once she dug at my mother's boils

with her nails. I know nothing of death
except for what the dead
have left me.

Gui Po – A ghost in the form of a kindly old woman,
who returns to help
around the house, and who was sometimes too close

to covet.

Her mother had ten pregnancies altogether. One was a stillbirth. One mouth less to feed, my mother remembers her saying. Below the full moon of the eighth lunar month, an open-air altar is set up for the worship of *Chang'e*, the Moon Goddess of Immortality. We are so stupid to worship the moon, my grandmother said. The Americans who went up there found nothing.

Her father was a Chinese physician. In his shop, jars of preserved seahorses, snakes, cockroaches, centipedes, millipedes. Poison to get rid of poison, her father said. My mother was promised that a sweet, preserved plum would follow each black mouthful of medicine.

His father died when he was seven. His father loved to drink, and always came home late. One day he collapsed in the bathroom of a restaurant. My father doesn't remember much. He remembers enjoying soft drinks, peanuts and cookies at the funeral. It was well attended, and he was caught up in the festivities. In the coffin, his father's face was dark and purple. It was a very large funeral, my father says.

Beside a large river, I tore the head off a quail, as instructed. The liver was reddish-brown, with no white spots, which meant the quail should have been healthy enough to eat, but I threw it into the river as soon as the boats left. The smell on my hands ran on for days. The first sound of rain reaching the jungle canopy was always far away enough for me to hope it was the wind. I heard later that one of my platoon-mates lost his machete in the rising mud. In the jungle I came to know a darkness full of noise, none of which I could recognise.

I want very much to smoke but I know my mother
thinks I've given it up. I put the kettle on and I tell her I am going
downstairs. After filling it is necessary to either

expand or expel. Minutes later I return upstairs
to find she has made the cup of tea for me.
My parents are not used to seeing me for such long periods

in the house. My father comes into the living room
and turns on the television.
This means he wants to listen to us, or at least

wants to be near us when we talk. Seeds
forgotten in
dew-soaked earth return as radiant things. I tell him

that his 'session' will take place
the next day because I don't want him
to feel neglected.

I. groped about in her father's pockets. There were two chocolate teddy bears, which she ate immediately. My sister and I would run to meet him on the patio at the front of the house, where he would be forced to reveal any gifts he had for us. Spilling his bags toward the living room. These gifts were simple, often chocolate or comic books, or – better – chewing gum and bubble gum, which were contraband items in Singapore. Good for once, I.'s father said to her. Good as good, she said in return. Years later, I realised that these gifts were gestures of affection, which he found otherwise difficult to express. Years later, I. had written a book, so he could give her a little place for pride.

After lunch my mother walks into the dining room
and my father and I both
blow our noses.

In the past when I thought about people my parents
were somehow
not among them. But some wound stayed

wide in all of us, and now I see in their faces
strange rivers and waterfalls, tilted over with broom.
You are watching the brown-paper covers of books grow

out around your father, as he dreams there
against the wall, thinking perhaps
how rocks are not quite lands.

My father works in a study at the front of the house, where he can see
only a portion of street, through the driveway's
mouth. I watch him dab his eye

with a tissue, the drooping eyelid no longer
able to adequately spread
and contain its fluid.

Last year, he fell against the stone
steps of his sister's house in Singapore, damaging the
nerves and muscles on one side

of his face. Some cultures consider crying to be
undignified. The Māori *tangi* involves the cultivation of intense
wetness around the eyes

and nose. In this expression of mourning, the wetness of living bodies
is invoked. Wet touch is closer and faster than dry touch. Sound travels
more quickly in water. So does electricity.

The air between me and my father is hung
with tiny water droplets.

I urge him through. I know that behind his answers
the memories trickle toward deep
cuts of anger.

Yuan Gui – a ghost who has died a wrongful death.
He roams the world of the living, waiting
for his grievances to be redressed. He hasn't left

anywhere he's been.

New Zealand Post rejected my father's application to be a mail sorter. He loves New Zealand, but says he finds it hard to elude the growing sense of his own uselessness. He is terrified of becoming a burden, unable to fuck, walk or even speak. At home in Auckland he is always at his computer. Every email he writes is copied to every friend he has. As a child he would climb the Flame of the Forest in his backyard. On the roof of the house, talking at strangers passing along the dirt road below, safe from dogs. I like to imagine him being mistaken for a chimney.

He wasn't as well-off as the other students, many of whom were from successful and prominent families. Some were accompanied by servants and bodyguards who waited for them during recess. He says the other students knew he wasn't worth knowing, but I know he wasn't poor. His family owned three hardware stores, and lived in the only brick-and-tile bungalow in the village. His grandmother owned a house near the city that was rented out to British soldiers. They had two housemaids. One eventually returned to her hometown in China. The other passed away in a rest home in Singapore.

They stung him with words, hit him from all sides at once, men who had worked with him for years. It didn't matter, didn't matter about Dad losing his promotion, I. told herself. The Singapore government had broken my father's rice bowl, giving his clients direct broking licences. There was no longer any need for him. His own investments, necessary to supplement his heavily reduced income, emptied themselves out underneath him. The starlings waited in the courtyard. When a sparrow hopped off with a large-sized crumb, they waylaid it, pecked it, grabbed its crumb and sent it off.

A large bag, to fit over his head and the gas heater. He woke the next morning, finding himself still alive. My father tells me he doesn't care much about having to leave, but I know he wishes he had a reason to stay. I have lived with reluctance sometimes, he says.

In his yelling I recall always hearing, 'what I've given', and 'respect'. He barely got out of bed, and if he did his head was fogged with anger and sadness. He hadn't noticed that years had leaked away between us. Coming back each night, late and drunk from entertaining clients. He had seemed more interested then in his dogs than his family. Because I wouldn't crawl to them, I. recalled her father saying. The stronger his desire to possess us, the further we withdrew from him.

I'm sorry I can't help you, I said, falling asleep against the deeply fissured wood in his eyes. I woke up in the middle of the night. He had fallen asleep gripping his shovel. By then all two or three hundred trenches held a candle at one end. We were all going to the same place.

My mother's voice is leaking
through the ceiling into
my room.

I know she's on Skype, because when she's on
Skype she speaks loudly.
My mother is speaking to Vivian, the sixth of nine.

Sitting next to Vivian is Bob, her husband. Karen, yes
you are my sister in New Zealand, Vivian says.

She giggles, and then is quiet.
My mother can see her already drifting out
under thick marsh.

Milk was left in buckets outside the classroom. It was feared that the students were undernourished. A drain nearby where my mother went to vomit if the milk were rancid. The school was very strict – very English, she says. Pleated, navy-blue pinafores, and bloomers. Once Vivian climbed a frangipani tree, hoping to leave school unnoticed. She caught herself on barbed wire, panicked, fell, and broke her arm. There was barbed wire and chicken wire everywhere, around all the churches, schools and houses. Barbed wire and chicken wire were much cheaper than fencing, my mother says.

There are wonderful gardens and flowers here
in New Zealand,
my mother says.

Vivian had been spending more and more of her time
in the garden, while Bob working in Cambodia
returned for only a few months

each year. The children, whom Vivian
had taken care of more or less
single-handedly, were studying and working

in England. My mother barely saw her
in the time leading up to our departure for
New Zealand.

The impact of each raindrop creates a small
crater in the soil, ejecting
soil particles up to five feet away.

Vivian became almost completely reclusive, leaving the house only for church on Sundays. She also began accusing another sister, Lorraine, who lived next door, of stealing from her. Cats were giving birth in her house, and my mother arrived one day to find the attic covered in blood and faeces. In France, they call an asylum *maison d'aliénés*. It is my own fault, I make my own bars, I. said. The outside an ache she had to curl herself around.

Three years after we moved
to New Zealand, Vivian was diagnosed with
Alzheimer's disease.

Bob takes care of her full-time now. She cannot
wash herself. She still enjoys caring for
simple plants around her house.

In Vivian's garden, the trees refuse
to stay fallen. There, to her,
the wind doesn't move

on to another place. She is
still there, hiding behind the heliconias, her face
beautiful as torn silk. Simply afraid,

she is already changed.

Goodbye. Vivian disappears. Bob disappears,
re-appears. I had to tell her exactly who
you were, he says to my mother.

Gu Hun Ye Gui – a ghost who has died
far from her family. She waits
for a kind person to guide her home. She never

wants to be seen, but likes the idea
of being found.

In 1926 I. arrived in Sydney under the pretence of seeing a specialist about her damaged knee. Her pregnancy borne of a loveless affair. Christopher Robin Hyde changed his mind about coming into the world. The little face I. touched was still warm, very dark, the mouth turned down. The eye is a region of calm weather, surrounded by a ring of thunderstorms. The houses of Sydney and its purple-dark faces crowded through long arcades. The iris is responsible for controlling the amount of light that can reach the retinal wall. Insufficient adaptation to dark environments is called night blindness. I. decided thereafter to write only under the child's name, Robin Hyde, knowing that he would be forgotten for her own safety. An eye within an eye.

I. was still in the hospital recovering from the stillbirth. I was at the gate with the other reconnaissance troops, waiting to board our plane for Thailand. His brother brought the news. Harry went to England, and died in Birmingham. The one who has to fly north, whether he wants to or not. He was twenty-one years old. On the phone I was told that he collapsed on a stair in a restaurant in New York. He was twenty-one years old. This hanging on with one hand, the other hand full of seas. An accumulation of fluid that produces swelling, and that sometimes eventuates in rupture.

I. stayed on D'Urville Island in the Marlborough Sounds until her pregnancy, the second, began to show. The family she boarded with took her on their next ferry ride to Picton. I won't know another safe day till you're out of the house, Mrs Snape said to her. At a lawyer's office in Blenheim, she asked whether she would be sent to prison for registering Derek as legitimate. My parents had gotten married in a hurry after Joel was conceived, a fact revealed to me and my siblings only after a particularly spiteful argument between my parents. My mother tearfully begged me to speak to Joel. At the time I couldn't understand the shame she felt.

We found them outside our classroom, on the walls by the grass. There were pencil sharpeners that could be bought cheaply from the school stationery store. These had a small plastic container attached that held pencil shavings. Most of us used these containers to house our spiders. I had a glass jar with a magnifying lid to keep mine in. The spiders we found were all more or less the same size, and I always thought they had the same face. The original intention was for them to fight and kill each other, but we struggled just to keep them alive. Even when we managed to put two of them together they often seemed uninterested in fighting. Once I saw that my spider had a sac of eggs attached to its abdomen.

Unable to support him financially, I. boarded Derek with an old Irish woman, Mrs Rattan, in Palmerston North. As Mrs Rattan rocked Derek in her arms and flashed her broken white teeth, I. was convinced of her kindness, and would pay Mrs Rattan £1 once a week for Derek's board. I first met my aunt Lyla when I was ten years old. She was my mother's youngest sister, given up at birth to a Muslim family. She wore a headscarf, and spoke with a different accent to her brothers and sisters. Until then I had had no knowledge of her. Aunt Lyla drifted in and out of contact with the others, before completely disappearing from them.

In under ten strokes, the first beginning from my right temple, I no longer had hair. I was moved from that large room to another large room for those without hair. While in the first room I had spoken to and learnt about some of the others, in the second room I found myself unable to recognise any of them. We were told to put on grey training singlets. We were told how to arrange the items in our lockers for inspections. Fifteen strangers asleep in one room that night. I thought that we all had the same face, that we all had the same eyes.

: a friend I have not heard of or from in over one year

: friend you have not heard of or from in over one year

: yes

: we would not be interested in helping you find him

The police representative looks sorry
although I find it hard to accept her words. Walking down
the steps of Wellington Central Police Station, I don't know

whether it was his being missing for over a year, or
whether it was his being a friend I had no evidence of
knowing.

Sometimes he thought it was a luxury
for him to feel too bad
to even be stupid. He often spoke to me

about buying nicer clothes.

[redacted] commented on your Wall post.

good. im staying here to regenerate my body... and my mind, my self. then i leave next summer. i had to give up my life in auckland but its worth it. need to consider that i will do next year... study maybe, but may switch to something else. have one book coming out soon, then i need to rethink my entire writing. Wellington is awesome, one of my best friends manages the [redacted] bar. go check it out.

Heavy glass doors to the left. I try to push my way in
but I need an access card. When I realise that cameras tilt
over this entrance I walk

directly to the receptionist. Mental health institutions
and hospitals
are some of the only buildings whose corridors and corners

must accommodate the length of a body lying horizontally.
From the receptionist I learn
that there is no centralised database for mental patients in New Zealand.

[redacted] sent you a message on Facebook.

Hi, how are you? I am staying at our family home in [redacted] bay, it is beside [redacted]. I have started working, in a cafe/bar. Some people consider it the best restaurant/bar/cafe in [redacted] so it is good. I had some barista training so do wait work. That is only on sundays, I started a month ago or so and am directing it to be a full time job over the summer. I am replacing my wardrobe, spending quite a bit of time into looking at good clothes for a good price. I have not done any writing since the beginning of this year, and actually recently was offered to write for a local paper. It goes out to over 5000 people so I have to consider what my article should be about. Then we will see if it will become recurring. There's many things I have been doing. And what are your plans? Are you going to continue studying in Auckland next year? I hope you are well too. [redacted]

The Salvation Army Territorial Headquarters
in Wellington has a tracing service
for missing persons. The man there

is young, and fumbles his words
before aligning them again. I know
that my friend is from [redacted] Bay

and that [redacted] Bay is beside [redacted].
I don't know his birth date although
I know he is one year older than me.

He always appeared
to me
to have walked a very long way,

even though he also always
appeared to me ashamed
of being nowhere.

Wu Tou Gui – a headless ghost who roams
aimlessly, who has gone missing for himself
in the way of missing something

he has never known.

[redacted] posted on your Wall.

I just wanted to say thank you for hanging out with me the times we spoke in Auck. I usually spend time with myself and I have had a lot of problems the last few years so thank you. Look forward to seeing where you go with your poetry.

In a dream I am holding hands with him
down a steep hill.

I. walked quietly out the door, down a long dark road. It was newly metalled. She sank down in the grasses, aware of her cut feet. At the medical centre, I instructed the soldier to urinate into a small plastic jar. He had been charged with drug use, and being away without official leave. He was required to report to the camp's duty officer every six hours. As I signed the tag on his urine sample, I tried to engage him in small talk, but he refused to look at or speak to me. I. was afraid of the doctor, and told him that she had been sleepwalking. It would be nice to think nobody would make scratches on this, said the matron, caressing the asylum's new safe.

I. waited until two boys had left the wharf. The heaviness of her body was a sweet heaviness. She let her hair swim out, was still and let the world flow around and into her. The black and healing silence of original possibility. She breathed in water. It is essential that amniotic fluid be breathed into the lungs in order for them to develop normally. When she was little she often ran away, finding somewhere to lie, face down in the wet grass. All she understood was that when she was in pain it wasn't confined to any particular place, but spread in great waves until it occupied every silver part of her.

Some of the patients found wandering the asylum grounds alone were quickly returned to the Main Building where they were locked up in their cells. I. used to cry for hours over these disappearances. On the *Changte*, on her way to China, she watched the Chinese ship-boys praying over the small tubs that held the tropical fishes they'd smuggled on board. Most of the fishes would not survive the journey to make their captors any money. On the boat, a woman she called 'Old Girl' kept her money pinned under her corset, its steel tips digging into her ribs and into the small and large of her back.

I was required to remember more quickly every time: I had a pair of wire cutters. There was a way of catching moonlight on the fence that I wanted to avoid. Sometimes I tried never to think about the past. Sometimes I tried always to think about the past. Alignment with the curve of the ground was necessary and I enjoyed the feeling of its curvature along the length of my body. I grew dizzy, vomited quietly in the grass, and the vomit warmed my shoulder. This is how we would get in, or, this is how we would get out.

I. didn't mind. It'd make her go to sleep. She wanted to go to sleep. The syringe jabbed down. Dull gold waves spreading all over the body. Full tide, quiet tide. A vast surf rushing up the sand with swirling driftwood and tiny shrimp in its throat, lemon leaves and sunlight dropping into it like tarnished coins. She touched the screw in her arm, and it was connected to every hinge in the universe. Outside her window, the trees collapsed, returning as toys, and she beat the toy trees with her toy hands. It was time to go to sleep. Don't go away yet, nurse, I. said. Little white face, black hair in small ringlets. Not yet cold to touch.

(The sea of Cora)

A moth darkens on the branch
of my mother's voice.
She is trying to winch me into the crying chair
but I am not crying. I am covered in yellow leaves.
My mother has moved into the back room where she hides her hands
folding laundry.
She raises the air in front of her body, steps wholly into it
and is gone.
The yellow leaves in the milk give it a rusty taste.

The box I stand on to reach the sink.
The water is cold.
I tell myself: Do not be afraid. It is already a secret.
I may have to lie down in this basket of unwashed towels.
I can hear my sister in the next room
laughing at the piano
before she begins to play a terrible sonata.
I close my eyes.

The rain is gone.
I open the window.
I make a friendly sign to my dog who is in the garden.
Downstairs I can hear
my father's voice unbuckle
swollen with darkness.
He says: Come out, I am growing old. I am aware that I might live here, alone.
I try to sweep the bark and the leaves
from my bedroom floor.
There is a tree growing at the back of my room.
I have loved it for a long time now
even though I have never seen it.
I touch leaves. It is difficult to move
or breathe.

There is a little house
under the dining table
that I live in.
Here I can eat apples
and sleep all day
dreaming of warmth.
It is just right for me.
No one can come inside unless I say so.
Outside the little house I can see
black-legged horses
rippling in moonlight.
They huddle together. I do not know them.
They have come to call me.
There is a cave in the space between their necks
that is bigger than I can believe.
It is an opening through which
I can be made to disappear.

I wake on scraped knees
and around me the night is creaturing.
Dark feathers bark
at windows.
A man with a beak
steps out of a nearby tree.
He strokes my hair with sharp hands
and flies up silently into darkness.
I want to cover my face with something soft
and the sound of my breathing that
goes on the whole time, under everything.

Someone has come out of the trees
holding her hands.
She is lashing softly on the grass.
I follow her over concertina wire into the pasture
where she has been grazing all day, alone.
Her antlers break apart in my hands.
We hold hands. We are friends.
We will follow each other into houses.
Now the trees are happy that we have
come back to them.
Leaves do not appear in the dark
and neither do we.

We are grass-footed.
My friend and I have left sadness behind us
crying in the dark branches.
Ahead of us is a field in which
we turn wide circles with our faces.
We are so happy to be here.
Now we are going to learn how
the moon's children
stand up suddenly
without breaking any shadows.
In the field we have buried bottles
filled with our hair.
We want to feel safe
so sometimes we just listen.
We have fallen out of the world.

Look, she says:
Nearby, strangers stalk
around a pond of silt and waste water
licking their pelts.
They are want and breath.
A man weeping for his past life
scrubs the back of his neck, the basin
choked with sleep.
A woman in her nightgown
crawls out of the trees.
She flies off
leaving her translucent skin
and a wall grows around her leaving.
Death is a house
inside the forest.
It is made of many
doors.

This is how you'll move now, she says
collecting stray pyjamas into a sail.
Your bed nailed to the bottom of this boat
where you sleep with yourself.
The forest is an endless sea and
the world turns in its dark waters.
You are not done with it.
The endless
trees out of which
everything emerges
and into which
everything escapes, and you
are covered in the leaves
of an emerging animal.
You are not yet done with it.
You fly out of the world. You go back.
The rocks here have been rounded
by that sound.

Wake now, it is time again.
There is a wide tooth comb floating in a jar of chlorine water.
When we get back from the hospital
the stones I've collected are still in the garden.
It's been a long stay.
Sparrows are falling out of my sister's hair
scattering their wings.
We feed them green jelly stolen from the ward.
We tell them: You must always come back to us.
The moon is still out there
pressed in its velvet box.

I. entered China in February 1938, with the Japanese military already occupying Shanghai and Nanking. It was common for air-raid signals to spiral through breakfast, followed by the thudding of bombs dropped in the distance. On the 8th of December 1941, the first Japanese bombs began to fall on Singapore. When the air-raid sirens rang out at 4.15 that morning, many thought it a drill, and the street lights remained on. She noticed how, in English, a hen clucks, a sheep bleats, a dog barks; but in Chinese, everything yells – a goat yells, a chicken yells, a child yells, and so on.

My parents didn't know about contraception. At the time, there was little or no sex education in schools, but they never considered giving up the baby. They were in love, my mother says, and knew they would marry. They left their church quietly. While registering for marriage without ceremony was becoming a trend in Singapore in 1975, both my parents' families were gracious in their support. There was a church wedding as well as a traditional Chinese wedding. I was still slim at the time, so no one else would have known, my mother says. During the tea ceremony, the bride and groom kneel in front of both sets of parents and serve them tea. The parents drink a small portion of the tea, and give them a red envelope, a symbol of good luck.

They first came to Wellington in 1976. My mother worked for the Bank of New Zealand while my father attended university. Joel, my brother and the eldest, was only a year old. My parents put him in a crèche run by the Sisters of Mercy, but my father skipped many lectures to spend as much time with him as possible. In the evenings he worked as a bartender at the Western Park Tavern on Tinakori Road.

I. had struggled with weeds and dank earth in another garden in another place, now taken away, but perhaps she could be more tender with this hillside patch. Laughing at her foreign-devil face in the mirror, above the sounds of drums and fire-crackers. She found that the few English people staying in the hotel wilted visibly when they met her. She knew she couldn't speak Chinese, and now she knew she couldn't speak English either. She was caught between two doors. In a dream, she watched a faceless friend leap silver patches of water, from one island to another.

You sound like you've eaten a lot of potato recently, he said. *Jiak kan tang* translates as 'eating potato', or 'potato eater'. This was an expression I heard often with regards to my accent. I. was caned for not getting pronunciation right in singing class. Swallowed a potato, have you, her teacher said. In New Zealand, it is sometimes indicated to me how good my English is. Who's marked or unmarked, or, who's marked as unmarked. When I look in a mirror I realise how I feel at home in anyone's eyes but mine.

From a little flat in Thorndon, they would invite some of my father's classmates around for dinner. Many of these students were younger and single. Many of them were from either Singapore or Malaysia. Disparate and disconnected elements have a tendency to resolve themselves in larger, more stable formations. My father says that my parents did have good local friends, but that they were few. As we are talking in his office he pauses to observe that I have had a much easier time. The way I speak and dress. It is strange to consider the difference between our differences.

An asylum's a place where people come when they have nowhere else to go, the doctor had said to her. Dashes between stationary trains, leaps up the sides of troop trains. In China, I. finally found a place from which she could stretch out giant hands, and make a road between two obscure villages. The good shoes that she had bought for walking the streets of Kobe in Japan were gone. Standing with water around my ankles at Island Bay, I wondered where those shoes went, and how, and what they did.

I. encountered a woman in Shanghai whose husband, a Chinese publisher, had been beheaded by the Japanese. In Singapore, Japanese secret police introduced the system of *Sook Ching*, which translates as 'purge through purification'. Those deemed anti-Japanese were gathered and taken to deserted spots on the island where they were systematically killed. The publisher's corpse was returned to the woman, but, headless, it was believed his spirit would wander, mutilated and shunned, for eternity. His widow fashioned a dummy head of wicker and clay. She hoped that this would allow his spirit to pass quietly into the afterlife.

The Hungry Ghost Festival occurs
on the fifteenth night
of the seventh lunar month.

During the Festival, rituals are performed
to appease the sufferings
of the dead. I make dinner and set the table

for an additional person.
I leave the seat
empty.

After dinner, I walk out of the house.
In Wilton's Bush, I can see the tracks
of small animals

running to and from the stream. I watch you
fold up water
from the stream, your face rippling

under pale wistaria. That unborn colour.
On this day the realm of the living lies open
to the realms of heaven and hell.

I find myself also reaching
for the places that empty
out beneath me.

Paper representations of material items
such as money, clothes and
houses are burnt as offerings

to ensure
that the deceased are comfortable
in the afterlife.

Are you back
from your wanderings yet? you write
in a letter to Harry.

Other rituals include releasing paper
boats and lanterns on water,
to ensure

that the ghosts find their way
back. I place five paper boats
in the stream. You gather them

downstream and somehow
send them
back to me.

Shui Gui – a ghost of one
who drowned, and who continues
living in the water. She tries

to gather the pleats around her
again and again
to sound out the whole.

Acknowledgements

I have lifted quotations and biographical facts, and adapted images and phrases, from the following published works of Robin Hyde –

A Home in This World. Auckland: Longman Paul, 1984.
Dragon Rampant. Auckland: New Women's Press, 1984.
The Godwits Fly. Auckland: Auckland University Press and Oxford University Press, 1974.
Young Knowledge: The Poems of Robin Hyde. Ed. Michele Leggott. Auckland: Auckland University Press, 2003.
Your Unselfish Kindness. Ed. Mary Edmond-Paul. Dunedin: Otago University Press, 2011.

– as well as from the biography by Gloria Rawlinson and Derek Challis, *The Book of Iris: A Life of Robin Hyde*. Auckland: Auckland University Press, 2002.

On page 25, the lines beginning 'Some cultures consider crying / to be undignified . . .' are adapted from Lisa Samuels' essay 'Membranism, Wet Gaps, Archipelago Poetics', in *Reading Room* issue 4 (2010), aucklandartgallery.com/library/reading-room-journal

On page 58, the lines 'She raises the air in front of her body, steps wholly into it / and is gone' are a variation on James Wright's 'and now she steps wholly into the air, now she is gone / Wholly, into the air' in his poem 'Beginning', in *The Branch Will Not Break*. Middletown: Wesleyan University Press, 1963.

On page 65, the lines 'Death is a house / inside the forest. / It is made of many / doors' are a variation on Claire Hero's 'Death is a house inside the forest. / Come. I am made of many doors', in her poem 'The Night was Animal', in *Sing, Mongrel*. Las Cruces: Noemi Press, 2009.

Personal correspondence has also been drawn on and used in the text.

This book is dedicated to my family. Thank you to Zarah Butcher-McGunnigle, Hera Lindsay Bird, Jessica Hansell, Louisa Kasza, Ross Brighton, Jarrad Dickson, Lauren Gould, Alice Miller, Lisa Samuels, Michele Leggott, Lynn Jenner, James Brown, Chris Price, Katrina Duncan, Anna Hodge and Iris Wilkinson, aka Robin Hyde.

First published 2016

Auckland University Press
University of Auckland
Private Bag 92019
Auckland 1142
New Zealand
www.press.auckland.ac.nz

ISBN 978 1 86940 845 9

Publication is kindly assisted by

creative nz
ARTS COUNCIL OF NEW ZEALAND TOI AOTEAROA

A catalogue record for this book is available from
the National Library of New Zealand

Cover design by Greg Simpson

Printed by Printlink Ltd, Wellington